Living Life with Death

Lessons Learned from the Death Industry

SARAH JONES

RESOURCE *Publications* • Eugene, Oregon

LIVING LIFE WITH DEATH
Lessons Learned from the Death Industry

Copyright © 2024 Sarah Jones. All rights reserved. Except for brief quotations in critical publications or reviews, no part of this book may be reproduced in any manner without prior written permission from the publisher. Write: Permissions, Wipf and Stock Publishers, 199 W. 8th Ave., Suite 3, Eugene, OR 97401.

Resource Publications
An Imprint of Wipf and Stock Publishers
199 W. 8th Ave., Suite 3
Eugene, OR 97401

www.wipfandstock.com

PAPERBACK ISBN: 979-8-3852-2923-9
HARDCOVER ISBN: 979-8-3852-2924-6
EBOOK ISBN: 979-8-3852-2925-3

10/10/24

To my dear Tristan, who listened to and loved my stories first.
I am glad you were my last date.

Contents

Preface | xi

PART 1   BODY REMOVALS

The First Body | 3

The First Embalming | 4

The First Removal | 5

Meet My Girlfriend | 6

I Know You | 7

Have Fun When You Can | 8

Chores | 9

It Didn't Go as Planned | 10

Too Hot to Handle | 11

Hello | 12

Psycho | 13

Extended Family | 14

Hazing | 15

Money Doesn't Buy Happiness | 16

She Sleeps Like the Dead | 17

Nap Time | 18

Squeeze | 19

I'm Not Ready | 21

Homeless Camp | 22

There Is Nothing to Fear | 24

Blame | 25

Don't Overthink It | 26

PART 2   TISSUE RECOVERY

First Recovery | 31

On a Date | 32

Too Close | 33

Eye Roll | 34

Splash | 35

On a Another Date | 36

The Lake | 37

Envy | 39

The Last Date | 40

ZZZ | 42

I Don't Know You | 43

PART 3   AUTOPSIES

The First Autopsy | 47

At a Party | 49

Why | 50

Perspective | 52

Bad Idea | 54

Fight | 55

The Fragility of Men | 56

Sorry, Kids | 57

Haven't Heard That One Before | 58

From Dust to Dust Indeed | 59

Lunch Time in the Morgue | 61

Did It Hurt? | 62

Hatred | 64
Can't Hide It | 65
Too Far | 67
Dirty | 68
My Side of the Table | 69
Heads Up | 70
The Last Body | 72

Preface

I attended a mortuary school in 2010 where I intended to become a licensed funeral director and embalmer. During my time in school I began working at a body donation to science program which involved transporting bodies from homes and scenes such as unexpected deaths, car accidents, homicides, etc. There was also an anatomy lab component to the job where I learned to do dissections.

I decided to leave mortuary school after a year as I knew the funeral home industry did not suit me. From there I learned about tissue recovery for donation and worked in that field for 5 years. After I had my son, on-call work became too strenuous and I took a break to focus on my kids. I moved into the role of autopsy technician once I returned to work.

This book is based off of my 10 years of death industry work. It is a work of creative non-fiction. Everything I wrote, I did experience but not necessarily in the same way I wrote about it. Some stories have details from several cases put into one or could be a compilation of my own and others experiences combined. I wrote it this way in order to protect the anonymity of the families that I came into contact with. This work is autobiographical but is not meant to be read as a biography. This work is much less about the dead people or what was happening around me and much more about my experience of being the person surrounded by it all. It is about my perspective and how I changed over those ten years. That being said any similarities to actual persons, living or dead (especially dead), is purely coincidental. Thank you for reading.

—Sarah Jones

Part 1

Body Removals

THE FIRST BODY

Ushered into the sterile room. Cold metal, pale tile, and dim lighting. A row of students stands shoulder to shoulder. Most look calm while my palms sweat. What if I faint or throw up? I don't want to seem weak. A hush spreads when the teacher enters and opens the small door letting out a gust of cold air. The reveal begins. Out comes long yellowed toe nails followed by skinny bent legs. Protruding hip bones and ribs form the top of a basin as the abdomen dips down, abnormally sunken. An algae green hue has started to bloom near the navel. Bruises and skin tears cover the arms revealing the ravages of time. The head comes out with its mouth hanging slack and open. His blue eyes are slightly shrunken and cloudy. I thought dead people were supposed to look like they were sleeping. They don't, they just look dead. It is an entirely unique state of being, a lack of being, a deep nothing. He smells like stale urine and stale person, it doesn't really make sense to me but makes it no less true. I stare, choosing fascination over fear. This is interesting. The snap of a latex glove pulls me from my thoughts. "Whelp, let's get to work."

THE FIRST EMBALMING

Fluid goes in, blood comes out.
Fluid goes in, blood comes out.
The pump of the machine is loud and the teacher has to yell as he works.
A slow ombre from white to pink ripples down to the long-yellowed toe nails.
Skin plumps as he is filled with artificial life.
The machine shuts off.
Holes are stuffed, organs are chopped, the body is washed.
Plastic caps cover cloudy eyes.
The jaw is wired shut.
No coming back now, it would be very uncomfortable for him.
Eyelids and lips are set in a pleasant way.
Now he doesn't look like he minds that he is dead.
Some powder here and a little color there and he is ready.
Now he looks like he is sleeping, all traces of the unpleasant hidden.
Stiff, pretty little doll.
All dressed up with no place to go.

THE FIRST REMOVAL

It is my first day. Let's see what this is all about. We pull up to the house. A very average looking house. The man is crumpled on the couch in the fetal position. He is wearing khaki pants and a button up shirt. It seems oddly formal. There are several family members waiting for us. They are friendly. There is a feeling of sadness but not desperation. He had been sick for a long time, this was expected. Perhaps a mercy. We ask if they would like to step out of the room while we move him. Most of them want to stay. Witnesses to my clumsy first body removal. We gently move the coffee table away, roll the gurney up to the couch and drop it down to the right height. He is lying on a sheet. I bend over his head and my partner bends over his feet. There is a black substance pouring from his mouth that has pooled around him. It looks like coffee grounds and stinks of blood and bile. I will discover later on in my career that this is one of the few smells that causes me to gag and here it is on day one. I attempt to stifle the reflex. I feel my stomach contract slightly while my eyes water. I stand for a quick gulp of fresh air and go back to it.

    We pull the edges of the sheet out and gently wrap them around the body creating a sling. We use the sheet to turn him on his back and carefully pull him over to the gurney. We strap him in, lift the gurney back up, and respectfully drape the blue velvet cot cover over him. The family travels with us to the front of the house. We open the door and pause. There is a long silence. We wait in the stillness with them. A soft symphony of rhythmic sniffling begins to play. Like water slowly dripping off stalactites in a cave. It does not disturb the quiet but enhances it. It belongs, the proper soundtrack for the situation. We wait a few moments more while staring down at our shoes.

    "Goodbye, Dad . . . "

    That's our cue. We walk to the van and load him up. We buckle in and drive back to our lives which have not changed, and leave them to their own which will never be quite the same.

MEET MY GIRLFRIEND

Cops surround the house so it is not hard to find. We pull in and enter the scene. The man lies dead upon the floor. My partner and I are planning our removal route when a mischievous face with a badge appears from around the corner.

"Hey, do you want to meet his girlfriend?"

I can tell from the sparkle in his eye and the bounce in his step that he has found a true treasure to share, so I follow. She is sitting on the corner of the bed, her back toward the door.

I can tell she is tall. Long blonde hair cascades like a waterfall to her tiny waist. She doesn't move as I enter uncertainly. The cop is wearing a wide grin.

"What should we name her?"

I turn to see her face. Blue flat eyes and a round, overly welcoming pink mouth greet me. Her legs are crossed at the ankles and her hands are delicately stacked on her lap. There is a gentle tilt of her head that creates the illusion of her being happy to see me.

Welcome home you! What should we do this evening?

I can't help but reach out and touch her inanimate arm (seems like the one safe place). She is soft but cold. She has a closet full of clothes, more than I could dream of. A cute vanity full of makeup, brushes, and jewelry await her in the corner.

"She looks like a Brittany to me." I reply.

"There is another one in the closet and we already named her Brittany." So, this is how the other half lives.

"What about Veronica?"

I KNOW YOU

Pager goes off.
White male age 22.
Pick him up, bring him in, you know what to do.
Stomp down to the morgue.
Drag him to the cot and off to the M.E. office we go.
Just a routine night, my partner and I laugh and joke as we drive.
Pull up, unload, wheel him in.
Cut the tag, open the bag as the attendant starts to check him in.
. . .
I see the ring on his left hand.
Married white male age 22.
Whose eyes are the same shade as the man asleep in my home.
Though it is hard to see them through all the crusted blood on his face.
They could have gone to high school together.
One future shattered while mine still stands.
I swallow the bitter knowledge that he could always be next.

HAVE FUN WHEN YOU CAN

Man fell off the bridge
His arm flew off. Who gets it?
Rock, paper, scissors

CHORES

Fridges full of parts
Heads, arms, legs, spines and torsos
Inventory day

IT DIDN'T GO AS PLANNED

Driving through the rough part of town. Lots of people are sleeping on street corners or just sitting taking long gulps from paper bags. We pull up to a small place. A row of duplexes. I cross through the narrow doorway. The power is not working, seems the bill hadn't been paid. It is dusk and the natural light is waning. The cops turn on their flashlights. It is a small studio, she is on the bed which is on the opposite wall from the door. The floor between us is a sea of garbage and there is danger lurking amongst the waves. Needles with brown blood on the tips glint gently when the light hits. I hope my boots are sturdy enough to withstand a potential puncture. The twenty feet we have to travel feels much farther. We begin to step lightly, crunching through the debris. I am hyper aware of my feet. We were told she is 60 but she looks 80. Her teeth are missing and she is highly wrinkled. Her dress is yanked up to her neck and there is nothing underneath. She must have been working when it happened. We decide to carry her out, we can't get the gurney through the mess. We bag her cautiously. There are more needles on the bed than there are on the floor and all I have is a thin pair of gloves. I don't get paid enough to get hepatitis. The cops diligently hold their flashlights so we can see our hands but do not volunteer to help. We carry her out in the bag. Luckily for us, she is malnourished. Maybe 90 pounds. We exit safely and load her up. I close the back door of the van. She lost this round of life. Hopefully her next one will be better.

TOO HOT TO HANDLE

House fire leaves charred remains.
The arms and legs end in sharp crumbling bone.
The rest has been burned away.
Everything is stiff and blackened.
Ash covers the scene.
The skull is brittle and cracks as the body is moved.
Chunks fall and the dry shrunken brain shows through.
The thighs have burst open from heat, juices run.
The body is easy to get into the bag, it is light.
We load up and drive.
A heavy silence blankets the car ride.
My partner, who is driving, shatters the stillness.
"Do you want to grab barbecue for lunch?"
"Oh yeah, that sounds good."

HELLO

I give him a wave
He grabs the dead man's wrist tight
and waves back at me

PSYCHO

The green puffed up man sits dead in his chair. Yet he is the least interesting thing in the room. I find myself in a house of curiosities. Naked hard plastic mannequins are set in seductive poses. Several walls are a mosaic of young female celebrities. Glossy photos cut from magazines overlap each other, shoddily held up by pins and tape. Some are attached to the head of a plain cardboard body. It looks homemade. Old boxes creatively carved into curvaceous female silhouettes. One wall is bereft of photos but catches the eye as light glints off of metal. Knives, swords, nunchucks, and throwing stars are displayed with pride. More celebrities smile at me with bleached teeth as I walk down the hallway. The closet is full of gray mannequin legs. Where do you go to bulk order plastic legs? Another closet is full of dolls in their original boxes.

The bedroom walls are pasted with pictures of a different kind of celebrity. Some are mildly suggestive and others make me feel like I need a shower. Disrobed Barbie dolls cover shelves and desks. More weapons litter the floor. I wander past the kitchen and see a dry erase board, it reads:

Jessica Reed Jessica Reed Ashley Grant Ashley Grant Jo Reynolds
Jessica Reed Jessica Reed Ashley Grant Ashley Grant Jo Reynolds
Jessica Reed Jessica Reed Ashley Grant Ashley Grant Jo Reynolds
Jessica Reed Jessica Reed Ashley Grant Ashley Grant Jo Reynolds

The names are written in an unsteady scrawl. Each woman has her own dedicated color.

My partner is looking for me. Before I go I quietly crack the fridge and freezer doors. There has to be a head or at least a severed foot in here somewhere. Nothing but frozen waffles and multiple half empty bottles of ranch dressing. I leave disappointed.

EXTENDED FAMILY

"So, your Mother told me what you are doing now."
    "You know, with the dead bodies and all."
    She whispers that part. I nod.
    "Well, I have a question for you."
    This should be good.
    "Why?"
    "There are a lot of job options sweetie. A LOT! Why in the world did you pick this one?!"
    Before I can answer she continues.
    "I just don't think that a young girl should be hanging out with (again she whispers) dead bodies."
    I ask her who should be hanging out with them.
    Her eyes go wide, "No one! No one should! What kind of question is that?!"
    I ask her what we should do with dead people if no one should ever be around them.
    "I don't even want to think about that!"
    I take the opportunity to explain that people like myself are the reason she doesn't have to.

HAZING

Dark murky water
What's in there? Reach in and see
All hail the new guy

MONEY DOESN'T BUY HAPPINESS

The house is massive. It is a mansion dressed up as a castle. The entry double doors are probably fifteen feet tall and each six feet wide. We won't have any trouble getting in and out. We push our cot through the grand foyer. Which I pronounce as FOYUR and they probably pronounce as FOYAY. Everything is classy yet ostentatious. 10X20 foot paintings hang on multiple walls. The crown molding is gilded. There are full sized suits of armor propped against the walls. I wonder if they come alive at night. I have no concept of the amount of money someone has to have to live like this. I only know it is copious. We walk the length of my house to get to the master bedroom. I am happy it is not on the second story.

The old man is sitting in his wheel chair. Most of him is slumped over. The rest of him is spattered against the wall. I assume he used a shotgun. His wife left to see a friend and came home to this unpleasant surprise. I run to the van to get some plastic bags. We can't leave anything behind. I pick up what is left of his brain and slip it into the bag. We scour the room picking up all the pieces from the floor and walls. It is not officially a competition but my partner and I keep side eyeing each other as we increase our speed. We will compare on the way back. We finish our Easter egg hunt and bag him up. I watch the massive house disappear as we drive away. For what does it profit a man to gain the whole world . . .

SHE SLEEPS LIKE THE DEAD

We enter the nursing home and approach the desk. The body is in room 25. We enter with the gurney between us. Two women occupy the room. There are no names listed but this won't be hard to figure out. We can easily tell which one is ours. We look back and forth. Both women are tiny and wrinkled. Both of their heads are tilted to the right with jaws slightly dropped. Their complexions are sallow and eyes only half way closed. We look at each other.

"Let's see who is cold."

We each gently touch one of their arms. I am careful, I do not want to scare the living one. They are both cold. We bend down toward them as we listen for breath.

"Anything?"

He shakes his head. I stare at him and he stares at me. We shrug in tandem. The nurse tells us it is the woman on the right. We bag her up and strap her in. As we are leaving I look at the woman on the left and whisper.

"See you soon."

NAP TIME

Night shift. I am on rotation to pick up bodies for the medical examiner's office tonight. It is 3am and I need a nap. There is a storage closet with three cots. They are less like military cots and more like beds you would expect to see in an insane asylum. They consist of a metal frame with short legs and the top is covered in small springs. A thin plastic mattress that is covered with a sheet lies on top. They are light and can fold up easily. I drag one out to the anatomy lab. It is a large square room filled with metal tanks. Each tank contains a body. The medical students dissect them all semester. The space between two tanks is perfect. I flop down on the cot nestled between the tanks. The room stinks like embalming fluid but they keep the temperature low which tamps down the smell. It is a cool metal cave. The cot smells stronger than the bodies and I don't know why. Whatever, I will sleep on my back. I set my pager where I can hear it and drift off to the droning hum of the a/c. I wake to the sound of lively voices and movement. Two medical students have entered with the intention of putting in extra study time. I lie still momentarily, unsure of what I should do in this situation. I don't want to startle them but I assume they will be more frightened if they turn the corner and see me. I sit up and the springs of the cot screech loudly. The students stop.

"What was that?!"

I try to get up quietly but the cot is squished between the tanks and I have to scoot to the edge causing the legs to scrape along the floor and the springs to squeak. While trying to move I open my mouth to let them know I am there but all that escapes is a loud yawn. By the time I stand up they are gone. I hear quick footsteps and distressed voices fading down the hallway. I look at my pager, 4am. Serves 'em right, damn over-achievers. Back to sleep I go.

SQUEEZE

We pull up to a small house. Cars line both sides of the street, leaving no space to park. We find an open spot 500 feet away. Is this the right place? We walk. People are sitting on lawns and blocking the sidewalks. We swerve and dart cutting through the masses like sharks on the hunt. People eye us suspiciously as if we don't belong. I suppose we don't. More eyes take notice of us the closer we get.

"Hey, where you goin'? You dun belong here." I lock eyes with the old man and point to the officers standing in front of the house. His gaze narrows. We walk on. We approach the officers, they look exasperated.

"Man, I'm glad you two are here. Get this body out of here so we can go. Where is your gurney?" Far away. An officer offers to accompany us. We walk back. The crowds realize we are there for a reason now.

"Why, do ya'll wear all black?"

"You ain't cops, why you here?"

I ignore them as I navigate the sea of bodies. Why are they all here? The crowd thins and the last 100 feet to the van offer us some breathing room.

"Don't these damn people have lives? This is ridiculous." I ask the officer if he has ever seen this before.

"Oh yeah, happens in neighborhoods like this where everyone is broke and bored. This is the event of the week. People will be asking at church; did you see what's his face? I watched them pull his dead body out of the house! Same reason people used to watch hangings, nothing better to do."

The sight of the gurney sends out a shock wave of excitement. Heads pop up over other's shoulders as they strain for a glimpse. Some reach out and touch the smooth vinyl where the dead man shall soon lay. I hope they will wash their hands. The officer walks in front of us waving wildly to shoo people off the path.

We finally enter the quiet safety of the house. The body is that of a young man. His tall frame is splayed across the bed. Money sticks out from under the mattress, and there is a gun nestled within a paper bag on the dresser. No obvious trauma, I assume it is an overdose. We bag him up, this is the easy part. The difficult part awaits us outside. The officer looks through the window. I throw out the idea of moving the van closer to the house.

"I wish you could. There are too many people in the street. We'll get you back."

My partner steps out first. The crowd erupts at the sight of him. One woman screams and falls forward onto her hands and knees. Several men cry and beat their chests. Another woman shouts prayers for the deceased with her hands pointed toward the sky. Wails and cries spread amongst the throng. One officer walks in front of us while the other two flank the gurney. They wave their arms about, put their hands out, and yell at those who get too close. The voyeurs continue to push in. Hands brush my back and shouts pierce my ears. Occasionally an arm shoots past me to grope at the body. It is too close, everyone is too close. The cacophony is overwhelming. I want out, I have to get out. They squeeze tighter and raise their voices. There is a threatening electricity in the air. The subtle crackle before lightning strikes. The officers get louder and are now grabbing shoulders to move people to the side. They feel the tension too. We are being choked, one more squeeze before the snake strikes. With sweat on the back of their necks the officers lower their right arms simultaneously until their hands hover above their firearms. It is enough. The crowd releases us and slowly slithers away, some back to their homes and some back to the street. We practically sprint the last fifty feet to the van and load up while our hands fumble. We drive away faster than we should. They will move this time.

I'M NOT READY

She answers the door
Tears stream heavy from her eyes
We give her more time

HOMELESS CAMP

We pull up to a large industrial building with a single cop car out front.
   "Follow me."
   Confused, we follow. We stop at a large wooded area.
   "In there?"
   He nods.
   "How far?"
   He laughs. This is gonna suck. We pull out the gurney and start our trek. The terrain is rough but I am grateful for a narrow trail to follow. We often have to lift the gurney and carry it over gnarled roots and rocks. It is a hot day and despite the shade of the trees I start to sweat. How much further? Suddenly the trees clear as we enter another world. Dozens of tents are set up in chaotic patterns. Laundry lines sag with the weight of dirt-stained clothing. We navigate through the maze of shelters. I can't help but survey the inside of every home we pass. Sleeping bags, pillows, blankets. Buckets filled with soapy water and sponges. Greasy fast food wrappers, cigarette butts, and empty beer cans are littered all over. We pass a cold fire pit with pots and pans scattered about. We found the dining hall. A tiny unknown town hidden amidst the shadows of the urban sprawl. There is a certain appeal to it, a sense of freedom. A glance into the past of when we used to hunt and gather. A modern form of living in the wild. Society demands order. Demands alarm clocks, deadlines, sacrificing times of fulfillment for a paycheck. We have to earn everything we own every day. Here, what you own, is what you own. No one here is paying off their tent. They wake, eat what they have, hunt for more when they need to and do as they wish in between. Of course, many of them are on drugs or struggling with mental illness. I do wonder if any of them chose this life. Perhaps, they made the decision to see the stars every night. To live with open hands feeling confident that they will be filled daily. Does anyone here feel like that? Or are the risks of violence and people avoiding their gaze better than the

alternatives our world offers them? Or is there just no way out? The body is lying in the creek. Looks like he was bathing himself and died of a heart attack or overdose. We secure the wet muddy bag on the gurney and away we go, back through the trees. I wonder how long it will be until eyes from our world will see this place again.

THERE IS NOTHING TO FEAR

The body is slumped against the wall. It is in an awkward position, we form our plan. A young officer, who has no idea what he is talking about, keeps giving us suggestions. His chest is puffed and he is full of bluster. We glance at each other trying not to roll our eyes. We each grab one of the dead man's boots and give a mighty heave. As he slides down the wall his body releases a long ghastly moan. Much like the sound someone makes after they have held their breathe for too long. It happens occasionally when air gets trapped in the lungs. We hear a door slam as the puffed-up police officer runs out of the house. He is shouting as he runs through the lawn toward his squad car in a panic. We look at each other and share a smug grin. New guy.

BLAME

We move the body
A smell wafts, I look over
"It was him, not me!"

DON'T OVERTHINK IT

We pull up to a beautiful house. Around back is a beautiful pool. It is a lovely final resting place. Sorry buddy, you can't rest here. He is floating a few inches from the bottom looking fairly peaceful. We can't reach him from the edges. We assess the situation. My partner leans over.

"I am not sure what the expectation is here but I refuse to swim in death juice."

I concur.

"Hey! You two, the fire department is on the way. Just hang out for a bit!"

We do so happily. My mind wanders, how will it work? I envision a 24-hour on-call specialist. The only guy to call in these situations. Tromping through the scene in full scuba gear, he somehow makes flippers look cool. "D.F.D. - For Dead Bodies Only" is printed on the suit in yellow letters. Yeah, that's how they will get the body out. I then kick around the idea of a trawl net attached to a motor. Maybe they just reel the body in like a tuna. What if there is an attachment that converts the truck into a giant crane game. Or a sleek black device labeled "Sonic Retrieval System." I have no idea what it would do but it seems like something that should exist. I hear a truck door slam. They're here! Four slightly doughy guys round the corner clad in . . . t-shirts? Their hands are empty. Where is the specialty equipment and the suits?! They stop at the edge of the pool and look down. One guy points a few times while speaking and they begin. Two of them grab pool skimmers. One hooks his skimmer underneath the dead guy's armpit. The other places his skimmer on the outside of the man's arm and they pinch them together. They have created giant chopsticks. Gently, they pull the noodle like body up to the surface and over to the edge of the pool. The body slowly floats along side them as they walk the perimeter to the shallow end. They each grab an arm and pull him to land. The whole process takes two minutes.

"There ya go, the rest is up to you."

Seriously?! I could have done that . . .

Part 2

Tissue Recovery

FIRST RECOVERY

65-year-old man. Heart attack. It is my first day of training for tissue recovery. It is also my first day experiencing the joy of working on-call. My first case is in a cold operating room suite at 2:30am. I keep yawning behind my face mask while I watch as the room is cleaned and covered in blue sterile drapes. The team scrubs up and carefully wraps themselves in gowns and slip on perfectly clean gloves. Nothing can get dirty. If something sterile goes outside of the sterile zone it must be discarded. They meticulously begin the recovery. They remove skin from the back, flip the body and remove skin from the front. It comes off in long thin strips and is stored in a solution that will keep it in good condition. After each tech sets up on one side of the body they pick up their scalpels. Incisions go down the arms and legs allowing bone and tendons to be removed one at a time. They are all wrapped, labeled, and stored separately. The team lead who is charting the information for the case scrubs up last and removes the corneas while the other two finish up. It is a well-oiled machine. The last item to recover is the heart. After the team lead completes the corneas she quickly moves to the chest. It is the first time I have seen a human heart. This man's is large but that is to be expected considering his heart disease. The heart is rinsed and packaged. Everything goes neatly in the cooler. That cooler contains skin capable of saving a severe burn victim from becoming septic. A new heart valve for someone with valve regurgitation. Tendons to repair an athlete's injury. Corneas that can restore someone's sight. Bones that can be shaped into many forms to help heal many problems. It is recycling at its finest. The process isn't pretty but the results are worthy. The team inserts prosthetics. They sew and shape the limbs back to their natural form. The funeral home does the rest. It is now 6:30am. A phone call comes in, we have another case to get to.

ON A DATE

On and on he drones until he remembers I am still sitting there.

"So, uh, tell me about what you do. Something medical right?"

I tell him.

"Oh, wow, okay. Uh, tell me more about that."

I recount my day. I had two recovery cases.

"Okay . . . so tissue recovery, what does that mean exactly?"

He speaks cautiously and his eyes flit nervously. I explain that we remove tissues such as bone, skin, tendons etc. He looks a little pale.

"Skin . . . oh okay. Like how? Do I want to know?"

I laugh and say it is up to him. I already know he is going to break but I am curious to see how much more he can handle. He laughs anxiously and claims he wants to know more. I explain a bit about the process, how we use a device called a dermatome which removes the top layers of the dermis. I speak cautiously and thoughtfully attempting to ease his discomfort. He is nodding his head quickly while trying to hold it together, he isn't doing well. I decide to end his suffering.

"It is pretty much a deli slicer, which is appropriate because the skin does look like deli sliced turkey."

That does it. He vigorously shakes his head and waves his hands.

"No, no, I'm done! I can't hear anymore!"

Well, he tried.

TOO CLOSE

I stroll down to the hospital morgue. Just a routine cornea removal. Should be a quick in and out. She is wrapped in a sheet on the table. Her little body is dressed in a simple t-shirt and jeans. It just lost its battle with brain cancer. As I write down her effects I notice her pockets are bulging. I reach in. She is still warm. Out fall dozens of small folded notes.

We love you.

Get well.

We miss you.

Pictures of flowers and hearts scribbled by well-meaning classmates. At the bottom of the pile is a picture. The little girl on the table, life still in her eyes, is grinning and hugging a woman next to her. The woman looks happy. There are mountains and blue skies in the background, maybe it was a ski trip. There is writing on the back:

My precious little girl

I am sorry, I wish I could have protected you.

I would have done anything to have saved you from this but I wasn't able to.

I am so sorry. I love you so much and I will never stop missing you.

I cry uncontrollably for 10 minutes. I have to get this case finished. I scrub up and begin. Her eyes are pretty. Her mom will never see them again. Tears threaten to fall once more. I choke them back. I don't want to mess up the recovery. I am packing up her corneas as the funeral director comes in to take her. I greet him, we smile and laugh about something inconsequential. I walk away pretending that nothing affects me.

EYE ROLL

"Watch closely students."

They huddle around the top of a table watching as she places drapes on the dead man's face.

"I am prepping for an enucleation, which is the removal of the entire eyeball."

She opens her kit. It is an old kit with an old instrument.

"Oh, look at this! It is an enucleation spoon! We don't use them anymore but I will try it today."

One student asks why they aren't used in recoveries anymore. She isn't sure. It is a spoon with one deep wide slit in the middle. When the eyeball is lifted she slips the spoon underneath sliding the optic nerve into the slot.

"See, isn't this neat? It holds the eye in place while I cut the rest of the nerves and musculature."

She has the students' full attention. She is almost finished. She goes to cut the last muscle that is keeping the eye attached to the socket.

Snip.

Her hand jerks ever so slightly. But it is enough. The eyeball is flung in a triumphant arc. Over her head, over the student's heads, and across the room. It lands with a soft squelch, bounces three times, and rolls under a table. All mouths hang agape.

"I guess that's why they don't use them anymore."

SPLASH

Swollen body lies
Waves flow down from the table
My socks squish for hours

ON ANOTHER DATE

"So, tell me about your job, I want to know more!"

I'm not sure what else he wants to know.

"Oh man, I have so many questions. Like, what is the bloodiest goriest thing you have ever seen?"

I throw out a recent homicide I worked.

"Wow, that is so cool! What about the grossest thing you have ever seen?"

I tell him about a particularly nasty decomp pick up. He is interested and engaged. I don't get to share my stories often. It is nice to have an audience. We go back and forth with questions and stories for a few more rounds.

"So, I have a serious question. This is something I have thought about a lot."

Okay.

"Like I have pictured myself seeing a dead body and have seriously wondered if other people would react like this."

He is acting weird.

"So, like, when you work on a body you have to undress them right?"

I don't like where this is going.

"So, and just hear me out, if there was like someone young and fit on your table. Like, I could understand someone being attracted to them, you know?

No, I do not know.

"I mean, not in a weird way."

How is that not weird?

"I'm just saying you have to have seen at least one hot dead body since you have been doing this."

I haven't.

It was nice while it lasted.

THE LAKE

It is a beautiful day.
Blue skies and soft waves.
Everyone runs and jumps into the water.
They play and splash.
Laughing and enjoying themselves.
I sit on the shore in a comfortable chair enjoying the breeze.
People pass by shouting at me to join in.
No, thank you.
I know too much of what these waters could conceal.
I have death on the brain.
I have pulled many bodies out of many lakes over the years.
They are heavy and unwieldily.
Full of fluid and caked in muddy vegetation.
There is a distinct smell to water deaths.
A commingling of lake, earth, fish, and death.
I am not scared of a body being in the lake.
I do not fear looking down into the water to see wide eyes and a pale face staring back at me from below the surface.
If I trip in the water I do not assume it is a severed human limb resting upon the silt.
I am not paranoid but feel confident there is a dead human in there somewhere.
I have too much experience with what leaks out of dead humans to consider swimming with them.
If there isn't one stuffed under a log somewhere there are plenty of dead animals in the water.
They leak too.
I can't stomach the idea of being fully submerged in potentially juice-filled waters.
That is an unfortunate downside of being around death all the time.
You know it is always there.

I am content to wave as the others pass by and read a book in my chair.
Perhaps dip my toes in occasionally.
Maybe time will blur my memory one day but until then I will wait for a pool.

ENVY

Hello.
> No answer.
> How are you?
> No answer.

Dead people are rude. I slowly get to work. I look at the wrinkled, withered face lying before me. What I wouldn't give to be you right now. I know I have recovered four cases but I've lost track of how long I have been working and I don't know how much more I have to go. My feet hurt from standing and my fingers are numb from holding scalpels. I just want to rest. And here you are throwing your own eternal rest in my face. I consider all my roles outside of this place as an attempt to bring myself back to a more positive mindset. My burden just feels heavier. I yearn to crawl onto that hard, cold table and allow the lights to go out. No more work, no more relationships, no more effort. I would never have to think of a witty reply, stand in line, wait in traffic, or be in this horrible room again. The thought becomes more and more attractive as the nuisances and pains of life pile upon me. No one asks anything of the dead and I have no more to give so it would suit me well. Life demands too much of us and I am weary. Death can't be too poor an alternative. I am around dead people all the time and have never heard a complaint. I fill my lungs. An unwelcome reminder that my heart will beat for the foreseeable future. Lines, traffic, and uncomfortable social interactions are still mine to bear. And who knows how many more of these damned dead people. I pick up my scalpel, which has never felt heavier, and begin. What is that line again? Something about miles and sleep...

THE LAST DATE

We sit across from each other at the narrow two-person booth. The restaurant is raucous with the sounds of music, clinking dinnerware, and loud conversation. I am surprised she wanted to go out to dinner with me. She just got off work. Eighteen hours of cases. Although, I would probably be hungry too after all that. Hopefully she isn't too tired and I will get to hear some good work stories. Her work stories are way more interesting than mine. We order our drinks. When we first met and she told me what she did for work, I thought it was really fascinating. How many people in the world get to do that? I am lucky enough to get to experience it second hand. I ask her what her day was like.

"Oh, we did four cases today. They were all local, which was nice, but that also means no car nap."

I can tell, she has dark circles under her eyes and has yawned several times already. She is telling me about the first case but cuts off when the waitress approaches. We order. Two cases were naturals and went by pretty quick. The other two were young, in their early twenties, and took much longer.

"Yeah, on the first one we had to take everything. He was only twenty and he hung himself which means all of his tissues were healthy. So, we took all the usual stuff plus tons of skin, veins, corneas, heart, and bone marrow. Bone marrow by itself can take an hour. It's horrible and boring. I just sit there and watch someone mess around with syringes. I almost fell asleep while I was sitting on the cooler."

I suggest she does next time as well. Our food arrives. I ask why the other one took so long.

"Oh, that one was long for a whole other reason. He was an absolute mess. It was a really bad car accident. He was so messed up we couldn't take anything from one side of his body."

I see our waitress walking towards us with a wide smile on her face.

"His left leg was completely smashed, like bones sticking out everywhere and it was almost completely severed underneath the knee."

The waitress is about two feet away from our booth and opens her mouth to speak.

"His thigh had this huge gash in it and it was the weirdest thing, his keys were stuck in the muscle. They must have been in his pocket and he was hit with such force that they got lodged into his leg."

The waitress's mouth slowly closes.

"They were deep in there too. I tried getting them out and I mean I pulled really hard. They were so tangled up in his musculature that they wouldn't budge and of course I'm getting blood everywhere trying to mess with it."

A subtle look of horror flickers across the waitress's face.

"So I gave up and just decided to cut the stupid things out."

The waitress turns and stiffly walks away.

"How's your steak?"

It tastes better with a good story.

"Mine is kind of bloody, but it's the least bloody thing I have seen all day, so I will take it."

She turns her face and side eyes me mischievously. I laugh. She offers me a warm smile. Her hand floats across the table and lands gently on top of mine.

"It's nice to have someone to talk to about this."

ZZZ

It is late at night
Our case lead puts on smooth jazz
Why does he hate us?

I DON'T KNOW YOU

We are heading to the medical examiner's office for an evening case. The sun is setting in magnificent sprays of pink and orange hues. I don't particularly want to be here. I have a 3-month-old baby at home and returned to work a week ago. Now I am on-call for an infant as well as the dead. In this particular moment I am on-call for a dead infant. This is my first baby case since my son was born. I exist in the opposite spectrums of life simultaneously. Anxiety festers within me. Less like butterflies and more like a swarm of bees. I don't know how I am going to react to seeing a baby on the table. We get our room set up and the team lead exits to get the child. Please don't look like mine, please don't look like mine, please don't look like mine. He returns and opens the tiny bag. I see a wild shock of black hair and dull hazel eyes. This one doesn't look like my bald blue-eyed one at home. As I exhale my shoulders relax and I scrub in. I recover the baby's tiny heart which fits in the palm of my hand. It will go to another baby now. I stare at the cold organ and think about my own baby. I am perfectly fine. Is it fine that I am fine? I don't feel a thing. I have four years of dead babies under my belt, is it just old hat now? Does this make me a professional? Perhaps becoming completely desensitized is to be expected.

People have asked, "What's wrong with you that you are able to do your job?"

This is the first time I find myself asking the same question.

Part 3

Autopsies

THE FIRST AUTOPSY

I am standing in a new morgue. They pretty much all look the same. Nonslip floors, dim fluorescent lighting, and lots of stainless steel. They all smell similarly too. This one smells stronger than usual. Someone is rotting in the fridge. I don't have to deal with that one quite yet. The one I am looking at is fairly fresh, died two days ago. A woman in her early sixties. She has short skinny limbs and a large drooping belly. Her saggy jowls give the impression she is displeased with her newly dead status.

Too bad. There is a lot that needs to be done before any cutting begins. Pictures are taken with clothes on and then clothes off. Height and weight are recorded. More photographs are taken of any wounds or bruising. All of her effects are documented. It looks like she died in bed. She came in wearing a large shirt with a pair of underwear and house slippers. The body is rolled to check the back. More pictures.

The doctor enters and examines the body notating any findings and then the tech gets to work. She cuts a Y shaped incision. Diagonal lines from each shoulder that meet at the sternum and one long line from the lower ribs down to the pelvis. The abdominal cavity is one of the few parts of the body I have not seen before. I lean in. She cuts deeper than I expected. There is a thick layer of fat, probably around eight inches deep. I can tell she was a smoker due to the fluorescent yellow color. The abdominal wall is peeled back and the intestines are exposed. A new scent fills the room. The chest plate comes off and the heart and lungs come out. The heart is large and the lungs are dingy with black speckles. No big deal, seen that before. Then she jumps down to the intestines two quick cuts and they are loose. She grabs the knotted mass and lifts them out with effort. They are heavy.

Next, she removes a large yellow colored liver. I wonder if it is supposed to look like that. I find out later that it is not. Stomach, kidneys, and adrenal glands are taken out in a flash. How does she do this so quickly? She starts working on the bladder. I am informed that in most circumstances the uterus and ovaries would be attached to it but this woman has had a hysterectomy. Good to know.

The body is mostly empty. I suspect she is finished until she pulls back the upper flap of skin on the chest and tucks her scalpel underneath it and up toward the jaw. She cuts in one smooth circular motion and pulls the tongue down and out through the neck. Two more flashes of the knife and the tongue, windpipe, and aorta, which runs most of the length of the spine, are removed in one long piece. That is new. Only the brain is left now. I have removed these before but it has been awhile. She makes one long incision starting from behind one ear lobe across the scalp to the other. The scalp is peeled forward over the face and she uses the saw to cut through the skull. A quick crack and the brain sits vulnerably. I see the scalpel move one, two, three times and it is out and cradled in her hands. The organs are weighed and the doctor begins dissecting them one at a time.

I look at the clock the whole process took her 16 minutes. For my sake I hope that is considered very fast. I can't imagine being able to do everything I just saw at that speed. The doctor says the liver is fatty which is why it is so soft and pale. He spouts off a few more findings and educational information. There is nothing suspicious. Cause of death: poor choices.

AT A PARTY

A pleasant conversation and then the question comes.
"What do you do?"
I always say medical, maybe I can dodge it.
She is interested and presses for more.
I tell her.
"Oh . . . well that is . . . different . . ."
I laugh and nod, hoping to break the tension.
There is an awkward silence between us.
She says she sees someone she knows.
I won't be seeing her again.

WHY

I pull the tiny bag from the fridge.
She took one breath and no more.
Dark wild hair tops an oblong head.
Her body is red and wrinkled.
Her form shows the traumas of birth.
The price that must be paid to enter the world.
All that work for one breath.
I think of her parents as I weigh and measure her limp body.
The loss of a child is more than just the loss of a loved one.
It is the loss of a future.
It is a crib that has no use and diapers that remain in boxes.
First steps that will never be seen.
There are beautiful dreams attached to a child that dies with them.
I take a few x-rays.
How many missed experiences?
It is not all bad though.
Life is a mixed bag.
So much beauty she will miss and so much pain she will be spared.
We are born, we live, and we die.
The moment we emerge the only thing we are guaranteed to do is die.
Whether it is after one breath, like her, or after 100 years.
It is something we will all do.
She ran her race quickly and hit the finish line early.
I doubt that is any comfort to her family.
They are the ones that have to live on with shattered dreams and broken hearts.
I pick up my scalpel and start to remove miniature organs.
I wish this examination would give them more peace than it will.
We can see if there are drugs in her system, we can see if she has a congenital defect or if she suffered violence.

We can find an infection.
In most infant cases there are no definitive answers.
We don't always know why things happen.
We usually don't know why things happen.

PERSPECTIVE

7:45am, bodies are prepped and ready. I sit and sip at the third cup of coffee held between my shaking hands. This is my one moment of quiet until we are finished for the day. I am halfway through this cup and already contemplating a fourth. My fellow tech comes in from the backdoor. The lingering cigar smoke wafts up my nostrils and mixes with the taste of my coffee. I watch him down a packet of B.C. powder, chug a can of soda, and place a wad of tobacco in his mouth. It is now 7:47am. Our manager walks in and asks what is on the docket for the day. Two naturals, a car accident, and a double homicide. She perks up and starts a barrage of questions. How many bullet wounds? Do they have any suspects? Where were they found? She is fairly new and still gets excited by these things. She also isn't the one who is going to have to dig all five bullets out. Without any prompting, she pivots the conversation to her new diet and exercise routine. She always says she refuses to be on one of our tables. I am tempted to tell her that she doesn't have much of a say in the matter but I decide to let her be. She cuts off at the sound of the front door. Someone comes to the window and I walk away. Dealing with the living is in her job description, not mine.

It is now 7:54am. I am in the break room and hear someone shuffle heavily through the door behind me. The doctor is in. He takes slow steps toward the table and places a white box down. I watch him fumble about and drip coffee on himself. He doesn't seem to know the lid on his travel mug is loose. His pale face and heavy lids give him away. He is clearly hung over. I open the box of donuts. Four of the dozen are gone. I see their remains on the doctor's shirt. He asks what is on the docket for the day and deflates with a long loud sigh at the mention of the double homicide. My manager walks in and sees the box. I can tell she is being seduced. She throws out all the language of someone who really wants a donut.

"I shouldn't, they are so bad for you, maybe if I only eat a salad for lunch . . ."

She is starting to spiral. The doctor rolls his eyes and aggressively grabs his fifth donut.

"We're all going to die from something!"

He swaggers away, smacking his hand on the door frame as he leaves. I can't decide if I just witnessed foolishness or an act of freedom. It is 8:05am, time to get started.

BAD IDEA

He wears suspenders
I pull them hard, too hard. SNAP
Blood speckles my face

FIGHT

They scream back and forth
He leaves with the gun. Bang. Drop.
Does this mean he won?

THE FRAGILITY OF MEN

Self-inflicted gunshot wound to the head.
He was 45 years old and lost his job.
Self-inflicted gunshot wound to the chest.
55 years old, recently diagnosed with cancer.
Hanging.
23 years old, his note read, "Tell that whore I didn't do this because of her."
Two gunshot wounds, one for her and one for him.
She wanted a divorce.
Jumped from the 20th floor.
16 years old, he lost the championship chess match.
Swerved into an 18-wheeler.
38 years old, lost all of his money in the stock market.
Drug overdose.
19 years old, he couldn't provide for a pregnant girlfriend.
Drank himself to death.
55-year-old veteran, he just couldn't live with himself any longer.
They hurt much more than they show.

SORRY, KIDS

Other kids run joyously across the parking lot but you still have to hold my hand.
Other kids get to splash around in full tubs but yours is only a few inches deep.
I cut your grapes in half for a year longer than I needed to.
I wouldn't let you get the ball that rolled into an empty street.
Stop running with food in your mouth!
Get down from that retaining wall!
Don't play next to the fireplace!
You stand smiling triumphantly at the top of the playground equipment.
My heart thumps loudly as I envision your brains on the ground after a fall.
You swim across the pool with clumsy proficiency and I cannot look away for a second.
I can see your little body floating limp on the bottom.
Grandma picks you up to take you for a fun weekend.
I image what it would be like to get the phone call.
"Hello, Mrs. Jones, I regret to inform you that there's been an accident."
I remember waking up every hour when you were a baby to check that you were alive.
I remember opening your door slowly with my hands shaking if you slept too long.
I always check the car seats twice.
I know I hold on too tight.
I know I have to let you experience the world.
I know the chances of any of these things happening is minute.
I am sorry that I experience the world the way I do.
But I can't handle the idea of any of these things happening to you.

HAVEN'T HEARD THAT ONE BEFORE

"What do you do?"

I break the news gently.

"Oh, wow . . . Well, I guess people are always DYING to see you! Am I right?"

He laughs uproariously. I laugh politely. I look around thinking there should be balloons and confetti raining down while a siren blares. Congratulations! You are the 500th person to tell that joke! I'm not sure what kind of prize I would give out.

FROM DUST TO DUST INDEED

I walk into the morgue and the smell pierces my nostrils. I know what is waiting for me today. I roll the table containing the greasy black bag into the morgue and suit up. I am covered in plastic and latex, only my neck is exposed. Once the bag is open I get the full scent-sation. It feels thick as I inhale it, it sticks to me. Cloying, heavy, and indescribable. Some people try to mask it but two bad smells does not a good smell make. Best thing to do is take a few big whiffs and let your nose go dead. Speaking of dead, he has been for quite a while. First they bloat. Then they melt. He is melting. Everything is a shade of green or grey, except for the friends he brought. From afar they look like white still piles but as you get closer you see they are alive. The human body is not much different than a dead whale in the ocean, the sharks arrive. It is a feeding frenzy. The pale grubs wriggle and squirm and fight. Trying to get closer to the part they want a taste of. Their mouths are so tiny that I can't see them but that maw is capable of burrowing through the skin to get to the juicy bits inside. They wriggle in and out of their tunnels. They almost look happy, like they are dancing. I supposed I would be happy if I could live inside my lunch as well.

    Removing the clothes is the worst part. They have to be peeled off slowly or else I risk slinging maggots and greasy fluids across the room, and possibly onto myself. Under every layer of clothing I find more happy wriggling. There are thousands, or at least a thousand. The clothes are surprisingly heavy. They are saturated with oils and grubs that I steal away from their meal to cruelly lock in a tied red bag. These will go back with the body. I truly hope no family member has ever wanted them back. There is skull showing, one side of his face has had the flesh picked clean. His eyes and most of his neck are gone and there are several large holes throughout the rest of the body. I cut through the slippery flesh and remove the ribs with a branch lopper. I think it is the same brand as the one in my garage. The organs are shriveled and dry. I remove rubbery lungs and shrunken kidneys. They look like bad movie props. The body cavity is lined with a coagulated substance. It looks like a mix of cold bacon fat and crystallized honey. I am cautious as I cut, my hands are slippery. I can feel the movement of the little creatures through my gloves. Only the brain is left to remove now, the saw groans as it is pushed through the bone. I preemptively grab the scale basin, I know what to expect. With the crack of the skull a dam has burst and out runs a sick gray gruel. I wish from dust to dust were true. But the reality is from goo to goo.

LUNCH TIME IN THE MORGUE

Fly lands on my lunch
I know where this fly was born
I still eat my lunch

DID IT HURT?

A folder slaps onto my desk.
Another homicide, third one this week.
I sigh heavily.
This is going to be a lot of work.
She is little.
Just six years old.
Her father is in custody.
There was a hammer involved.
I can't tell what her face looks like until I see her smiling image on the news.
As I undress her the full picture of the brutality is revealed.
Cuts, bruises, broken bits.
Dark shadows left from angry fists.
Some hits were to kill and others to be cruel but I can't tell which came first.
I hope it was the former.
I picture her in the house screaming and no one else is there.
How many hits from a hammer does it take to make the screaming stop?
1, 5, 10? I guess it depends on where you are hitting.
How many times was she able to plead no, why, or I'm sorry Daddy?
How long does one-minute feel when you are screaming and bleeding?
My heart rips and I desperately wish I could have scooped her up.
I don't want her to be alone.
Alone, afraid, in pain.
How much did she feel?
At what point does God wrench the soul from a tortured body?
A small soul that doesn't understand what she did to make her father so angry.
A man does as he will so there is no point in asking him why.
But to God I ask, were you there?

Did you comfort, did you shield, did you take her somewhere far
 away from the sound of her own body breaking?
I have not wept for the dead for many years.
For her I do.
Not now, later.
For now, I have work to do.

HATRED

A stack full of folders sits upon my desk. I peruse the cases. Two possible O.D.s and three naturals. Not a bad line up for a Monday morning. I fetch the first O.D. and start prepping. He has foam on his mouth and horrible teeth, probably a meth-head. I slip his shirt off. He has decorated himself with swastikas and S.S. insignia. I see these types of tattoos often. They are no longer surprising but always disappointing. I remove the rest of his clothing and finish taking pictures. I flip him over to examine his back. Oh wow, this guy has something that surprises me, and disgusts me. The tattoo covers his entire back. It features two beautiful Native American women. Their dark flowing hair is adorned with feathers. That is where the beauty ends. Their arms are raised above their heads. Shackles are clasped around their wrists. Their bodies hang limp and their heads are heavy. They are naked from the waist up. From the waist down they are nothing. Both women have been severed below the belly button. Their intestines dangle and drip as they intermingle. The backdrop of the gruesome scene is a rippling confederate flag. I don't know what is more disturbing. A person willing to paint their body in hatred or the painter willing to participate. The world may be better off.

CAN'T HIDE IT

There is only one folder on my desk this morning. I am giddy with the promise of an easy day. I skip to the freezer and see my case. All my good feelings quickly melt into a puddle of disappointment. A pair of large flaking feet are sticking out from the bag. The bag is zipped from the head down to the hips and looks like it could burst open at any second. I don't know who is in there but they have ruined my day. My back and hamstrings complain as I navigate the cumbersome table to the scale. I throw my whole weight against the table and manage to roll it up the small ramp. 500 pounds is the total after I subtract the weight of the table which is roughly 100 pounds on its own. Back down we go and into the morgue. I travel slowly to avoid slamming into every wall I pass. I take my first set of pictures. Time to undress him. Luckily for me people of this size usually wear minimum clothing. I only have a pair of shorts to contend with. I lift his trunk-like leg with one hand while pulling down on the waist band of the shorts and repeat the process with the other leg. My hands come away covered in white dander. His lower legs are dry and reptilian. They crack and bleed and weep yellow fluid. The skin that hangs from his massive belly is raw and open. Red angry lines cover most of his body. The skin is screaming as it is pulled, desperately attempting to accommodate his form. I need another person to help roll him as he threatens to fall off the narrow table and take us to the grave with him. Time to get cutting. I stand on the largest stool and his stomach is still at the level of my chest. It takes three deep cuts to get through his outer layer. The organs are huge. Before doing autopsies I did not realize that our organs continue to grow with our bodies after childhood. So much is being asked of them they need a means of keeping up. I feel bad for the man. It must be miserable being trapped in a prison of your own making. It is a sickness that cannot be hid. Bottles can be stashed in closets and tiny baggies of powder hid in sock drawers. He had to wear his ailment, his way of dealing with life's troubles and pains. People probably judged him at first glance. I might have been one of them depending on the day. He suffered while people stared. There is no need to be cruel to those who are different. Existing as they are is cruel enough.

TOO FAR

Homicide. Single gunshot wound to the chest. It is a rare instance of a wife shooting her husband. It is usually the other way around. The Doctor enters and we begin. I carefully make my incision around the bullet wound. I cut through the ribs and remove the chest plate. There is a gaping hole in the sternum. The chest cavity is filled with blood. I ladle the dark clotted substance out one scoop at a time. He has close to two liters in total. It is quickly obvious why there is so much.

"He was shot right through the heart."

I lift up the heart while it is still attached. A perfect bullet shaped hole in the center. The rest of the organ is split and shredded. She nods and gives me the go ahead to remove it. She starts humming on the way back to her station. I recognize the tune and start mumbling the words.

"Oh, you're a loaded gun, yeah."

The Doctor picks up quietly.

"Oh, there's nowhere to run."

A loud voice drifts from across the room.

"No one can save me, the damage is done."

We all belt out in unison.

"Shot through the heart and you're to blame! You give love a bad name!"

DIRTY

Thick dark gunk is packed underneath long nails. They extend out from his greasy hands. I can smell them from afar. Tiny brown roaches skitter across his knobby arms and legs. His toe nails curl and twist resembling burnt corn chips. Every inch of skin is speckled with crumbs, food wrappers, and pet fur. Weeks of sweat and oils form a strong mortar. He was rotting before he died. A sore the size of my fist gapes open revealing bone and sinew. He provided the microbes a tasty meal. It radiates a putrid essence. Dingy clothes are removed and bed bugs scuttle away when disturbed. I bundle his body bag up tightly to trap all the creatures before throwing it away. Several colonies survive the genocide by taking shelter amongst his wispy strands of hair. I spray down the table and scrub at dirt and dried fecal matter clinging to him. It runs down the length of his thighs. More soap and muscle are required. He is clean enough for the doctor to examine. Probably the cleanest he has been in months. My skin still itches and crawls at the thought of him for the rest of the day.

MY SIDE OF THE TABLE

Suicide, gunshot wound to the head, 43-year-old male. He was a cop. Several officers attend the autopsy to ensure there was no foul play. These officers do not know the dead man personally but they do know him. They are him. All of them wear a haunted veneer. Not a look that says how could he do it? But a look that considers, could it have been me? I wonder if any of them have ever experienced starring down the barrel of their own gun or pressed cold metal to their temple. Found themselves being pulled out to sea by the riptide of overwhelm. Weariness, whether emotional or physical can drive a person mad. I deal with stench, decay, and gore. I have the easy job. They deal with tears, angry words, and fresh crime scenes that may or may not be abandoned. I go home at five. They may not make it home. We are both like sponges absorbing sadness and the dark facets of humanity. A sponge has to be rung out or else it becomes saturated and can hold no more. It could happen to anyone. A mistake of pride. I can take it, nothing disturbs me! We all have our limits. I only see the results of devastation. I am not a witness to the moment. I am a cosmic janitor dealing with all the empty candy wrappers that have been left behind. I will stick with my side of the table, thank you. I can't fathom telling mothers their sons are dead. The outside is loud and chaotic. I like my quiet, predictable morgue. I always know what to expect of the dead. The living are bunch of wild cards. The doctor agrees it is probably a suicide. The officers sigh and nod their heads. Not everyone makes it.

HEADS UP

It is her first day in the morgue. I show her tools, labels, and case folders. Our current case is a car accident. The blue body bag is streaked with dull dried blood. Must be a bad one. She flits around excitedly and asks if she can open the bag. I snap a picture of the tag and give her the green light to proceed. She cuts it and unzips the top. As she lifts the flap her eyes are bright and glittering with anticipation. A quick glance and she snaps the bag shut. Her face is flat and still as if made of glass.

"He has no head."

Her words are quick and hushed. I laugh, it has to be in there somewhere. I walk to the head of the table (where there supposedly is no head). I lift the flap. She is right, the head is not where it should be. Ah, found it! I throw the bag open and point to it. The body is a mass of pulp and shards. Plastic, glass, and gravel litter the body bag and stick out of squishy bits. The head, which is actually the head, neck, right shoulder and right arm all in one piece is squeezed in next to his waist. I don an extra pair of thick gloves and grab under the arm. I pull, already feeling tiny shards poking through. They make my skin itch. The mass weighs close to thirty pounds and lacks rigidity. Every bone is broken, even the skull and face are a formless mass. It is difficult to find a productive place for my other hand. It is like moving a sack of sand covered in quills. A sand-u-pine. I piece him back together as best I can. I trace the fault line and show her that it matches where his seat belt would have crossed his body.

"I had no idea that could happen."

People tend to think they are sturdy but they really aren't. Being at the top of the food chain gives us the privilege of deluding ourselves into thinking we are strong but we are physically weak. It is our minds and imaginations that allow us to create layers meant to separate our soft bodies from the rest of the world. We encase ourselves in protection because we do not have any of our own. Clothing, buildings, cars, walls. We always have something to hide behind, it makes us feel safe, even if it is silly. During the cold war children were told to hide under their desks in case of a nuclear attack.

Ridiculous.

We tell ourselves a lovely lie so we can live in the delusion that we will magically survive fatal circumstances. We prefer the fantasy land to sitting with the reality of our finite and fragile nature. If a nuclear bomb breaks through the defenses of a building or if a 25-ton truck breaks through the defenses of 1.5-ton car the inside of this body bag is the result. It is the harsh reality of having no control.

THE LAST BODY

"Today is my last day and you sir, are my last autopsy!"
"I hope you feel honored."
Nothing? Dead people are still rude.
I weigh him and wheel the table into the morgue.
It feels like a normal day.
I process, I cut, the doctor does her thing and just like that, it is over.
My last body.
I place the bag full of cut up organs into the chest cavity and start sewing him back up.
It feels a bit surreal.
He is looking at me, I read his face as scrutinizing.
I'm sorry! I have to go back to the land of the living!
There is something else I am meant to be doing now.
I fit his skull back together and flip his scalp back over it.
One stitch to secure it.
I am a little scared to be honest.
What if I don't remember how to function in that world anymore?
I dispose of my scalpel blade and place all of the dirty instruments in a bucket of soapy water.
I take a sudsy towel and wipe down my bone saw.
Living people are messy.
I notice the bloody cutting board and scale and then glance at the body.
Well, I guess you are too.
I only have to deal with four breathers in this office and that is enough for things to get complicated.
I don't like emotional complications.
I start spraying the dried blood and small chunks left behind from the dissection with the hose.
The back splash, cutting board, and cutting board stand get lathered up and set in the sink.

People are messy and they are sensitive.
They don't like to know about the land of the dead and most don't understand those of us who travel there willingly.
I remove the grate, this is where everything that has fallen collects.
The remains of the day.
It all gets rinsed into the drain and the chute is cleaned.
All the suds are washed away and equipment is put back as it was.
I remove the instruments from the bucket.
They are rinsed and placed back on the cutting board.
The station is ready for whomever comes after me.
I won't be disturbing it again.
I will need to be cautious about what I reveal out there in the world.
It is difficult watching someone's eyes fall from sparkling interest to a flat and distant gaze.
They put on a polite mask, it is a poor attempt at hiding discomfort.
I wipe down the body and the outside of the body bag.
I throw the sack containing his property down by his feet.
The zipper of the body bag hums while it closes.
A faint consideration comes to me.
When will be the next time I will see another dead body?
It occurs to me that the next one I will see will belong to someone I love.
I consider the list of possibilities.
It will be strange when that happens.
I have never experienced seeing a dead body that was important to me.
I guess that is civilian life.
Another new experience.
The refrigerator door releases a puff of cold air as I roll his table into the empty space where he will wait for the funeral home to pick him up.
Whelp, goodbye.
I don't think I can say it's been fun.

I fill the mop bucket and roll it over to the station that is no longer mine.
There were some fun times though and funny times.
I wring out the mop.
And sad times.
The mop and I swish back and forth rhythmically.
Together we erase the last evidence of my day's work.
Frustrating times.
Exhausting times.
Confusing times.
I dump the water and put the bucket back in its little corner.
But it was always interesting.
I walk to the door and turn off the lights.
I learned a lot.
Dead people have a way about them, a wordless wisdom.
The door creaks softly and latches shut.

Printed in the USA
CPSIA information can be obtained
at www.ICGtesting.com
CBHW071152051224
18498CB00013B/474